HOW TO LIVE YOUR BEST LIFE

Live a Life You Love and Find Joy and Fulfilment Every Day

Sophie Golding

HOW TO LIVE YOUR BEST LIFE

Copyright © Summersdale Publishers Ltd, 2023

All rights reserved.

Text by Helen Brocklehurst

No part of this book may be reproduced by any means, nor transmitted, nor translated into a machine language, without the written permission of the publishers.

Condition of Sale
This book is sold subject to the condition that it shall not, by way of trade or otherwise, be lent, resold, hired out or otherwise circulated in any form of binding or cover other than that in which it is published and without a similar condition including this condition being imposed on the subsequent purchaser.

An Hachette UK Company
www.hachette.co.uk

Vie Books, an imprint of Summersdale Publishers Ltd
Part of Octopus Publishing Group Limited
Carmelite House
50 Victoria Embankment
LONDON
EC4Y 0DZ
UK

www.summersdale.com

Printed and bound in China

ISBN: 978-1-80007-936-6

Substantial discounts on bulk quantities of Summersdale books are available to corporations, professional associations and other organizations. For details contact general enquiries: telephone: +44 (0) 1243 771107 or email: enquiries@summersdale.com.

CONTENTS

INTRODUCTION

You only get one shot at life, so why not try to make it the best you can? No one is born knowing what their best life looks like – this is something that you only begin to piece together as you grow and experience the world. By working through the bite-sized tips in this book you can start to visualize what leading a full and happy life means for you as an individual, and how to go about making it a reality.

No matter who you are, living a life you love involves making intentional choices – it's not something that happens entirely by chance! Many of the quotes in this book are from famous people whose wisdom has been gained from overcoming life's challenges. Living your best life is about working out what will make you happy and embracing a way of life that makes you feel like the best version of yourself.

CHAPTER ONE

WHAT DOES MY BEST LIFE LOOK LIKE?

It's impossible to plan a life perfectly. Perhaps all the people around you seem certain of what they want, yet you feel less sure of your goals. Or maybe you're wondering how your life ended up this way. You can't know what your future might hold, and it will be full of unexpected twists and turns, but with a vision for the life you want to lead, you will start to feel more in control, more confident and more purposeful. Read on to help visualize your goals, work out your values and learn what your best life could feel like.

Create the highest, grandest vision possible for your life, because you become what you believe.

Oprah Winfrey

LIFE
SATISFACTION

Start with the end in mind. Imagine you're
nearing the last weeks of your life and
you begin reflecting. What things are you
proud of having achieved? What things
and people really matter to you now? What
things do you regret never having done?
Experiences can feel very different in the
present moment to the way you might reflect
on them with hindsight, so being happy in
the short term doesn't necessarily mean
being contented in the long term. Don't
wait until the end of your life to take stock.
Simply imagine what you want your life to
look like and start making it a reality.

Follow your passions,
follow your heart,
and the things you
need will come.

Elizabeth Taylor

FIND YOUR VALUES

Are you living your own life, or the life that someone else wants you to live? Knowing what your values are will help you set yourself goals that are meaningful and will be the force that powers the things you're doing. If your actions are truly motivated by your inner desires, you will be leading your best life.

Maybe what matters to you is learning new things or helping other people; being creative or spending time with family; feeling secure or nurturing your spiritual side. Try the below task.

1   Choose three to five values that resonate with what drives you, what brings you contentment and who you want to be as a person.

2   Next do a value audit to see if the way you're currently living your life aligns with these values. Write down three big recent purchases and three things you're currently pursuing.

3   Based on the values you've chosen, are you spending your money and your time in the right ways? If not, what steps can you take to adjust?

DON'T COMPARE YOURSELF TO OTHERS

It's hard not to use other people's lives as the benchmark for judging your own but when you compare yourself to your siblings or your friends, what do you stand to gain? All too often, it can leave you with feelings of bitterness, envy or even complacency, none of which are helpful. When imagining what your best life looks like, do not waste energy on comparing yourself to others. When you use yourself as the benchmark and try to do a little better than you did before, you will always be proud of your growth and achievements.

Compare yourself
to yourself

DO A LIFE AUDIT

At certain times, specific aspects of your life may take priority, such as when you're looking for a new job, getting married, caring for others, focusing on your health or starting a family. A life audit is a useful way to think about where you are right now in your life, and to identify the elements you want to work on.

Imagine your life as a wheel, like the one below, with seven different areas that are personal to you.

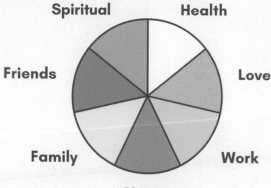

Spiritual   Health

Friends   Love

Family   Work

Money

Sometimes you will find certain areas of the wheel influence each other, like work and money. When you're living your best life, all of these areas will feel well balanced. You will feel healthy and secure, loved by those who matter most to you and at one with the world around you. Rate each area of your life on a scale of 1–10 and choose the two areas most in need of improvement to work on. Visualize what you would need to do in those areas to score a ten.

To accomplish great
things, we must
not only act,

but also dream;
not only plan,
but also believe.

Anatole France

VISUALIZE YOUR FUTURE

Once you've completed your audit and assessed the areas of your life that need attention, use a visualization strategy to boost your effectiveness, confidence and motivation. This means training your brain to imagine what you want to achieve in your future as if it were already present. You can create a vision board to help with this exercise – a collection of images that represent your desired result. Try visualizing both the outcome and the process by which you're going to achieve it in as much sensory detail as possible.

If a vision board doesn't appeal, the imagination is just as good and is commonly used by athletes to enhance their performance: for example, before a tennis game you might visualize serving into the box, imagining the weight and feel of the ball in your hand, how you throw it into the air, and the weight and speed of your racquet as it makes contact. Imagine how you feel when you score a winning point. To be effective, this mental technique needs to be practised regularly, so try visualizing when you wake up and before you go to sleep.

CHANGE YOUR PERSPECTIVE

Think about how you see yourself, then about how others may perceive you. The framing you give to a situation will always determine how you feel about it – including the way you see yourself. Is the queue in town an annoyance, or the chance to chat to a stranger? If things go wrong in an exam, you can choose whether to brand yourself a failure or see it as an opportunity for learning. When reviewing different elements of your life, remember things are usually not good or bad in themselves, but the way you look at them can make them appear that way.

Change how you
see and see how
you change.

Zen proverb

STAY CONNECTED

Are you outgoing and sociable? Or perhaps you're more cautious about social encounters because they sometimes drain your energy? People socialize in different ways, some preferring to be part of a group and others preferring to spend time with one person. You might also have a preferred method of communication – online, in person, over the phone, by text. Recognize what works best for you but then be disciplined about maintaining your social relationships. Invest time in people who will be a solid foundation for your best life. Having a few true friends that you can ask for help in any situation is better for your well-being than a huge network.

Choose people
who lift you up.

Michelle Obama

FIND YOUR IKIGAI

Ikigai is the Japanese concept of happiness rooted in the idea that you live your best life by doing something you love. This idea of a life of purpose and meaning is a bit like the French idea of a *raison d'être* - the thing that makes life worth living.

Write a list of things under the following headings: what you love, what you care about, what the world needs and work you can get paid for. Ikigai sits at the intersection between these four areas. Accomplishing something of value that you're passionate about brings contentment, fulfilment and the motivation to continue. Can you find your ikigai?

What gives you pleasure and joy?
Let those be the things that
lead you forward in life.

Julianne Moore

DO A TIME AUDIT

There will be many things you want to achieve in your life and even if you can do anything, you won't have time to do everything. Now is the moment to reconsider how you're spending the hours in your day. Starting with your values, and then the priorities you identified from your life audit, think about how you can schedule time into your week so that you make a commitment contract with yourself to give time to them. You're doing this because you've identified them as things that matter! Consider how you've lost time this week and think about how you can address recurring time-drains.

It is not enough
to be busy...
The question is: what
are we busy about?

Henry David Thoreau

WHY YOU WORK

Doing work you don't enjoy can leave you feeling demoralized and dissatisfied with your life. Start by asking yourself why you work. The writer Elizabeth Gilbert makes the distinction between a job, a career and a vocation. A job is something you do simply to earn money and pay the bills, but it does not define you; a career is a job you're passionate about and want to grow and develop; and a vocation is your calling or life's purpose. Framing your work in these terms can give you a better perspective on where you are now and provide the bridge to doing work you love.

Unpaid work such as being a student, looking after children, caring for elderly relatives or volunteering within your community has huge social and economic value. The International Labour Organization estimates unpaid care work to be worth around 13 per cent of global GDP, or gross domestic product (when calculated on the basis of the minimum wage), with women doing three quarters of this work. Whether your work is paid or unpaid, ask yourself if it's aligned with your passions. Is it giving you the opportunity for mastery? Look for work that gives you the freedom you want.

The meaning of life
is to find your gift.

The purpose of life
is to give it away.

Pablo Picasso

Do what you love,
and love what you do

GET GOING

It's great to have goals and ambitions but to live your best life you need the right motivation. This means having both the impetus to get going, and the power to keep going, no matter what, in order to achieve your goals. Things like money, power and the approval of others are extrinsic motivators – rewards from the world. As many celebrities discover to their cost, fame and fortune don't necessarily bring happiness. In contrast, curiosity, passion, purpose, autonomy and mastery are intrinsic motivators, which come from within. Focus on the intrinsic motivators you're in control of and you're more likely to set beneficial goals and feel satisfied with your achievements.

Don't wait.
The time will never
be just right.

Napoleon Hill

I am enough

LET GO

The mind coach Peter Crone suggests asking yourself a simple question: if you had no memory, what would your problem be? If there would be no problem, then you know your ability to live your best life is being hindered by your past. When faced with a challenge or obstacle, focus on future-facing, positive outcomes, and not the negative experiences of the past. You could try using a visualization technique (see pages 18–19). You can't change the experiences you've had but you can change how they will affect your future. Often you can learn from them and use them for personal growth – remember, they do not define your future.

I am the author
of my story

FINDING FLOW

Studies have shown that people who score the highest for overall life satisfaction are people with most flow in their lives. Flow is an optimal state of consciousness where we perform at our best and feel at our best. All of us are biologically hardwired to achieve a state of peak performance. Think of a time when you experience those moments of total absorption, when you're absolutely focused on the task at hand and the world around you seems to disappear. You lose all sense of time. In such moments the brain can produce all sorts of pleasure-and-performance-enhancing hormones.

To achieve more flow in your life, try to find a balance between the skills you have and a place slightly outside of your comfort zone. Getting this challenge–skills balance right means you will pay optimal attention to the task at hand. Doing work or a hobby that gives you regular access to a "flow state" is a great way to improve your well-being and life satisfaction.

The world needs
that special gift
that only you have.

Marie Forleo

CHAPTER TWO

HAPPY MIND, HAPPY LIFE

Being happy in yourself requires a healthy mindset and positive self-talk. The difference between daydreaming and making your dreams a reality is all in the mind. Believing in yourself and talking to yourself like a supportive friend means you can respond in the best way possible to whatever challenges may lie ahead. If a positive mindset doesn't come naturally to you, simply following the tips in this chapter could be life-changing. The ideas that you will find here will help you stay present and connected, keep a healthy perspective and build the confidence to accomplish your goals.

BEING YOURSELF

Being yourself means being in tune with your values and living authentically. While it's great to have role models and aspirations, emulating others can leave you feeling inadequate. Firstly, know yourself. Start by recognizing that no one else has your unique set of experiences and perspectives – this means you will bring enormous value to any job, friendship or relationship just by being yourself. And better still, no one else can be you as well as you can!

Secondly, attune yourself to experiences that always seem to exhaust or drain you – these are often indicators that you're having to put on a performance, rather than being truly yourself. Thirdly, it's good to push yourself out of your comfort zone occasionally, but the jobs and relationships that are right for you should build your self-esteem, leaving you feeling confident, valued and able to be your best self.

STAY POSITIVE

People who think the best will happen, rather than fearing the worst, have been shown to have better mental and physical health, as well as better immune function. Optimists are likely to respond better to stressful situations, so over time stress is less likely to damage their health. If confronted by negative thoughts, try positive self-talk, such as "I can do it differently", "I'll give it another go", or "I can learn something new". When you're talking to yourself, think about how you'd talk to a friend if you were trying to encourage them. Be kind to yourself and seek out positive people and positive habits to reinforce this thinking.

Nothing is impossible.
The word itself says
"I'm possible!"

Audrey Hepburn

GIVING
APPROVAL

How often do you find yourself
looking for the approval of others? It's
good to ask for the opinions of people
we value but sometimes there might be
someone in our life – maybe a parent,
boss or partner – whose criticism stings
the most. It may be that even if they
aren't present and haven't given an
opinion, they are dictating the decisions
you make because you constantly
have their critical voice in your head.
To live your best life, you need to
break free of this voice. Check
in with yourself for approval –
your opinion of you is more
important than anyone else's.

The only approval
I need is my own

BE PRESENT

Noticing the little things, such as the rustle of leaves or the trill of a bird call, instantly connects you with the present moment. When your senses are tuned into the world around you, your focus is on the here and now. It's hard to worry about what might happen in the future or dwell on memories of the past when you're fully absorbed in the present.

This is especially important at times when you feel anxious or overwhelmed. Focusing on your immediate environment can help distract you from feelings of anxiety and uncertainty.

The 5-4-3-2-1 grounding technique will quickly reconnect you with the present. Take a moment to look around you and notice:

- 5 things you can see
- 4 things you can touch
- 3 things you can hear
- 2 things you can smell
- 1 thing you can taste

Place your hand on your chest and feel your heartbeat, feel the solidity of the ground beneath your feet or the touch of the clothes against your skin. It may help to hold something in your hands while you do this exercise and feel its texture and colour, its weight and shape.

Past and future are

in the mind only –

I am now.

Sri Nisargadatta Maharaj

FINDING HAPPINESS

If you're looking to other people or material things to make you happy, chances are that true happiness will remain elusive. The things that give you instant gratification now aren't necessarily the same things that will cause you to look back upon your life with satisfaction and pride. This is because lived experience isn't the same as remembered experience. Living your best life is about living by your values, doing meaningful work and finding your purpose. Happiness isn't a destination but the result of everyday contentment.

Learn to let go.
That is the key to happiness.

Buddha

SEE THE GOOD

Looking for the good in every day and in everyone will make you happier and those around you happier too. Seize each new day as an opportunity to start afresh. Rather than waiting until you lose something to realize its value, carry out a daily audit by finishing the day with a gratitude journal. This is an effective way of reframing your day's experiences and focusing on the good. Gratitude can be infectious, so if someone has done something you're grateful for, remember to thank them.

Every day may
not be good,
but there's something
good in every day.

Alice Morse Earle

FINDING BALANCE

In a roughly balanced day, you might work for eight hours, sleep for eight hours, do everyday chores for four hours and have four hours of leisure time. When your workload increases, you will usually end up paying with this leisure time. The everyday chores still need to be done, and you still need to sleep, so a 12-hour workday can leave you without any time to catch up with friends, loved ones or to exercise. If you have young children, you might find yourself sleeping a lot less and doing a lot more chores!

A perfect work-life balance is an elusive ideal but try to schedule time to exercise and time to spend with the people who are most important to you. Set a policy of not answering work emails after a certain time and setting downtime on your phone an hour before bedtime. Once you set work-life boundaries and respect them yourself, others are more likely to respect them too.

SAYING NO

There are only 24 hours in a day, so every time you say "yes" to something you don't want to do, you reduce the time available for doing things that matter. Setting boundaries and saying "no" can benefit all areas of your life – from your health to your career or relationships – and ultimately prevent burnout. Be clear on your values and priorities and meet your goals and needs rather than other people's. If it's hard to say no, ask yourself why: are you afraid of disappointing others, or seeming rude? Do you naturally try to please everyone? Rehearse some polite ways to say no and be confident about taking back control of your time.

It's only by saying "no" that you can concentrate on the things that are really important.

Steve Jobs

STAY GROUNDED

When things go well, it's important to stay humble – don't let success go to your head. And conversely, when things go badly, try to keep a positive frame of mind. Both success and failure will pass, so the important thing is to stay focused on your next move. No matter what the outcome was yesterday, start each new morning afresh with confidence, focus and a positive attitude towards what you want to achieve.

Today is the first day
of the rest of my life

BUILD CONFIDENCE

Between your comfort zone and something that is outright terrifying, like a serious phobia, you will have a whole spectrum of fears and uncertainties. Fear will cause a surge in your body's stress hormones regardless of the trigger. Whether your worst fear is heights, spiders or speaking in public, the process of gaining confidence is broadly the same: start in your comfort zone and move outwards in small, safe steps.

For example, if you're terrified of public speaking, start by practising it by yourself in a relaxed state. Then in front of one person who you feel safe with and supported by. Then two or three friends, and so on, moving yourself gradually towards a situation in which there is a larger group, including people who don't know you.

This process, known as "systematic desensitization", was created by psychiatrist Joseph Wolpe in 1958. Practising relaxation techniques as part of the process can help you counter your fears, because your body can't be both relaxed and fearful at the same time. If you have a serious phobia, you should consult a therapist to help you with this process, but you can try the steps yourself for building your confidence and alleviating mild to moderate anxiety.

I am strong.

I am brave.

I am fearless.

BE KIND
TO YOURSELF

"If you don't have anything nice to say, don't say anything at all" is a phrase you might be familiar with from your childhood. But it applies to your grown-up self too. Being as kind to yourself as you would be to your best friend can be hard to do, but self-compassion is vital for resilience. This is all about forgiving yourself when you make a mistake, encouraging yourself when you feel like giving up, and looking after yourself when you've taken on too much. To live your best life, you need to make a conscious effort to eliminate negative self-talk and start loving yourself a little bit at a time.

Be happy with being you. Love your flaws. Own your quirks.

Ariana Grande

TAKE ACTION

There is a difference between knowing something and experiencing it. We say something is "easier said than done" because taking action can be challenging and sometimes risky. Yet most things can only ever be properly learned by "doing". Don't put off the changes you need to make in order to live your best life. If you find you're procrastinating – aimlessly using your phone as an escape or doing things you wouldn't normally want to do – ask yourself why, then think about the benefits those positive changes will bring to your life and find the courage to just do it.

I believe in
the power of now

BE PROACTIVE

Having to respond to situations you're not prepared for is highly stressful, which is why being proactive is the best way to take control of your life. Of course, many things in life are out of your control, but being proactive is about controlling the things you can. Good preparation is one of the best ways to do this. Scenario-planning before you make a decision, doing the pre-work before a meeting, packing your bag the night before, revising before an exam or taking an umbrella when it's forecast to rain are all classic examples of good planning.

If you're prone to procrastination, make an effort to put the time in straight away. Most tasks will take the same amount of time whenever you do them, so meeting deadlines, spending time with others or maintaining your responsibilities without hesitation is often much quicker than dealing with the fallout if you ignore them.

How wonderful it is that
nobody need wait a single
moment before starting
to improve the world.

Anne Frank

SELF-ESTEEM

If you ask someone about your best qualities, what would they say? It's easy to get so hung up on your own shortcomings that you don't see or value in yourself the things that other people do. Try not to rely on factors like body image, career success or money to define your self-worth. Such things can bring a welcome boost of confidence in the short term but are rarely the qualities that good relationships are built on. Whether it's helping out, being a good listener, making people laugh or offering good advice, make note of what other people value in you and take stock of these qualities in yourself.

Self-care isn't selfish.

It's self esteem.

Ashley Judd

SLEEP MORE

Sleep is perhaps the most important thing you can do for your health and well-being, and yet it's often the first thing that's sacrificed when life gets busy. Good nutrition is vital but if you sleep badly, you will probably feel too tired to exercise. Sleep boosts your immune system and has a huge impact on mood and your ability to cope on a tough day. Become aware of your sleeping habits by using a sleep tracker or keeping a written record. Avoid losing sleep during the week only to lay in on the weekend. By keeping your waking time and bedtime consistent, you will improve the quality of your sleep.

CHAPTER THREE

LOVE LIVING IN YOUR WORLD

You've evaluated the different areas of your life and what needs attention, so now is the time to implement some practical changes in order to achieve that change. Over the next few pages you will find new ways of thinking about your home and friendships, love and relationships, money and work. You will also find tips on nurturing your physical health and making lasting improvements to your lifestyle by replacing bad habits with good ones. Most importantly, you will have the chance to reflect on how you can spend your free time most enjoyably, learn the life-changing power of showing compassion and discover how to bring more purpose to your everyday life.

I am unstoppable

Be yourself;
everyone else
is already taken.

Oscar Wilde

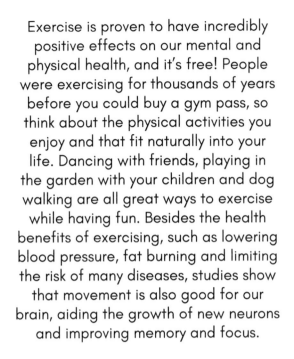

Exercise is proven to have incredibly positive effects on our mental and physical health, and it's free! People were exercising for thousands of years before you could buy a gym pass, so think about the physical activities you enjoy and that fit naturally into your life. Dancing with friends, playing in the garden with your children and dog walking are all great ways to exercise while having fun. Besides the health benefits of exercising, such as lowering blood pressure, fat burning and limiting the risk of many diseases, studies show that movement is also good for our brain, aiding the growth of new neurons and improving memory and focus.

Exercise has a huge benefit for our mood, thanks to our own internal pharmacy. Your body may produce endorphins, a hormone that works to reduce pain (rather like a natural opiate) and dopamine, which increases pleasure and encourages repeat behaviours. It also produces molecules called endocannabinoids (causing a similar effect to cannabis), which can help regulate mood and promote better sleep. When you work your muscles, you're also setting into motion chemicals called myokines that strengthen cardiovascular health and your immune system. Scientists have called them "hope molecules" because recent studies have shown they are highly effective in countering depression.

MAKE A HOME

Having somewhere you can call home isn't just about a building and its contents, however tastefully chosen. How you live in your house is what makes it your home, and this is almost certainly different from the way previous occupants will have lived in it or the way it will be inhabited a hundred years from now. Think of your home as a continual work in progress – a reflection of the different stages of your life and your present preoccupations. A home should be your private space, free from the worries of the outside world – a place in which you can truly be yourself.

Have nothing in your houses that you do not know to be useful or believe to be beautiful.

William Morris

GROW
YOUR GIFT

According to an old saying, talent is finding easy what most people find hard, and genius is finding easy what talent finds hard. While genius is truly rare, you probably have a talent you can nurture. Going with the flow of your talent is easier than trying to swim upstream – that's why it's such a gift! When something feels effortless, you might mistakenly assume it comes easily to others too, so take a moment to recognize and credit yourself with the things you're good at. It's great for your self-esteem, so factor into your life space to practise any skills that you're gifted at.

Don't wait.
Use your gifts!

TYPES OF LOVE

Love is a great influence on how we live our best lives, but it can also be complex and confusing at times. You might love chocolate but this means a totally different thing from loving your parents, which is different again from loving your partner. The ancient Greeks defined seven kinds of love. *Eros* is love of the body and sexual passion; *agape* is a selfless love for others with acts of charity and kindness; *philia* is the deep friendship we might have with someone like-minded; *ludus* is a playful, flirtatious kind of love; *pragma* is the long-standing love that develops in marriage and other long-term relationships; *philautia* is love of yourself, necessary for healthy self-esteem; and *storge* is the natural love of a parent for a child, or a child for their parent.

Typically, romantic relationships start with *eros* and *ludus*, developing towards *pragma* and *agape*. These types of love are healthy and necessary, but don't expect one person to be able to offer them all. They say it takes a village to raise a child, and in the same way, we need a whole network of relationships to love and feel loved. By understanding love's many forms, we can ensure that the love we give and receive adds to us having the best life we can.

Love has nothing to
do with what you are
expecting to get –

only with what you are expecting to give – which is everything.

Katharine Hepburn

FAMILY

While you're an individual, you're nonetheless inseparable from your family relationships. In the 1960s, psychoanalyst Murray Bowen developed "family systems therapy", which viewed the family as an emotional unit and applied "systems thinking" to an individual's behaviour. The way you communicate, frame situations and behave can be a result of a cascade effect down the generations. Consider how your position within your family (for example, being the eldest or youngest child), and the network of relationships between family members, may have influenced your life. This could offer you a new lens through which to assess not only past influences, but how they continue to affect you now.

I accept my family
just as they are

MIND-WANDERING

If you have a task-oriented mindset, the chances are you might find it difficult to rest. With an endless to-do list and a sense of needing to get things done to achieve your goals, you may struggle with the idea of doing nothing. Yet studies suggest that rest could be almost as important to our well-being as sleep and can help to raise our productivity. Mind-wandering, often defined as task-unrelated thought, is similar to daydreaming and can be a very positive form of mindfulness.

It has been shown to create more activity in the default-mode network of our minds, helping them recharge and reset. This is very different from the idea of mind-wandering as an unwelcome distraction or of having our mind hijacked by negative internal thoughts and ruminations. For busy or anxious people, a racing mind can make rest very difficult to achieve. In these cases, teaching your mind to rest and wander slowly and safely may involve some deliberate meditative effort. Although everyone will find different things restful, it seems that solitary activities, like reading, gardening or walking, are often necessary to restore peace and calm.

Studies show that spending time in nature is hugely beneficial to physiological and psychological well-being. The threshold at which people are known to benefit is two hours a week, spread across multiple occasions or all in one go. There are many reasons why green spaces have such a powerful effect on mental health, from the smells and sounds of the environment, a sense of calm or slower pace, to the connection with the seasons and the wider world. Spending time in parks, forests, the countryside, or walking by the sea, could introduce clarity into the life you want to live, or enable you to discover new things in familiar places.

Just living is not enough... one must have sunshine, freedom, and a little flower.

Hans Christian Andersen

Breathe in the
world around you

Almost everything will work again if you unplug it for a few minutes... including you.

Anne Lamott

SWITCH OFF

In this digital age, technology is designed to command your attention and is extraordinarily successful in doing so, affecting one's ability to be present and prioritize one's time. Yet avoiding the distraction of pinging emails and social-media notifications requires a discipline akin to an art form. Create boundaries and stick to them, ensuring that technology is working for you, rather than the other way around. Delete the apps you don't need from your phone; turn off all non-essential notifications; schedule downtime. For example, make a rule never to have your phone in your bedroom. These boundaries will significantly help you apply yourself without interruption.

There is always time
if you make it

CREATE

Whether you consider yourself a creative type or not, humans are all born with a problem-solving mind. Creative thinking can be seen in the way footballers create space and passing opportunities on the pitch, in the work of composers and lyricists or in the work of innovators and entrepreneurs. By solving a problem or making something new, you're doing the very thing that you're designed to do.

In today's world it's so easy to consume that you can forget to create, and as much as we are born with these skills, we also need to keep exercising our creative muscles in order to strengthen them. Don't be put off by thinking you need to create things to a professional standard. A simple daily creative practice such as journaling can generate meaningful personal insights, which may in turn lead to a valuable change in the way you live your life. A creative mindset is about finding flow and enjoying the process. It's also about giving yourself permission to make mistakes without fear of getting it wrong.

COMPASSION TO OTHERS

At the heart of any community is a strong network of social relationships. Helping within our local community – whether shopping for an elderly neighbour, listening to children read at the local school or being part of a local group – has obvious benefits for the whole of society. Now studies suggest that connecting with your local community has extraordinary health benefits for you as the giver, potentially increasing your quality of life, helping you live longer and reducing the risks of depression. So – do yourself a favour by doing something for someone else.

When we help ourselves,
we find moments of happiness.
When we help others, we find
lasting fulfilment.

Simon Sinek

FRIENDSHIP

Imagine your life as a train. Friends will hop on and off at various stops along your journey, and some friends will travel a long way with you. There is an old saying that people come into our lives "for a reason, a season or a lifetime". You need many types of friendships: the new friends who will show you who you are now, and the old friends who will keep you rooted. You will need different friends for different reasons but make sure your friendships give you energy and help you to grow into the best version of yourself.

Kindness is
contagious –
pass it on

DAILY RITUALS

The little things count. On their own they may appear trivial, but over time they accumulate into something bigger than you could ever achieve in a short while and can play a significant role in your life. This is as true of bad habits as it is of good ones. In fact, some of the habits that are most insidious may seem out of our control, like negative self-talk, toxic friendships and a permanent state of stress. Often bad habits might be so embedded that you don't even recognize them as habits at all!

Check in with your values and think about the habits that could help you live a fulfilling life. This could be practising a daily meditation, keeping a diary or setting a regular bedtime. Start by increasing your awareness of the things you want to change. Kicking bad habits is always hard, so think about how to replace that action with a new positive habit. Rather than focusing on what you should give up, focus attention instead on building something beneficial into your life, like taking microbreaks or giving more time to a hobby where you can use your talent.

Practice isn't the thing

you do once you're good.

*It's the thing
you do that
makes you good.*

Malcolm Gladwell

EAT HEALTHY,
LIVE HEALTHY

While it's true that burning more calories than you eat leads to weight loss, fixating on calories can result in some poor health choices. There may be fewer calories in a packet of crisps than an avocado, but there is significantly less nutritional benefit. Depending on your goals, seek advice on adapting your diet to meet your needs – for example, wholegrains are great for fibre, organic yoghurt for calcium, or certain nuts for protein. Instead of calorie-watching, think about the food journey from producer to plate and which ingredients are less processed and closest to their natural form. The meals you cook from scratch are likely to be much healthier.

Feeling confident, being comfortable in your own skin – that's what really makes you beautiful.

Bobbi Brown

MAKE SPACE

Arrange the contents of your home to work best for you. Clearing out old papers, clothes you never wear, or unused gifts will create space, a sense of order and maybe even a sense of calm. If you're trying to create better habits, organize your space in such a way that the things you need to use regularly are visible and easily accessible. Frame favourite photos and display the things that bring you joy. Discard anything that is no longer relevant in your life and make more visible those things that are in accordance with your goals and values.

Without change,
nothing changes

BREATHE

When experiencing changes in life, it's easy to feel overwhelmed, which is why it's important to know some tools to help with self-regulation. Breathing can be used to increase your awareness of how you're feeling in the present moment.

When you think about your breathing, you're taking control of what is usually an automatic process. This sends a message back to your brain that you can control other involuntary responses, like stress and anxiety. The heart and lungs are linked to a network in the brain that controls automatic bodily functions. When you breathe deeply, you activate the vagus nerve, which releases a chemical messenger, helping to lower your heart rate. This allows your body to calm down.

Box breathing is an easy technique to remember and practise:

- Breathe in for four seconds
- Hold for four seconds
- Breathe out for four seconds
- Hold for four seconds

Repeat this cycle until you feel calm and relaxed.

Practise box breathing daily, ideally for a couple of minutes at a time and at different points throughout the day. By introducing this effective micro-habit into your daily life, you will feel grounded and prepared to tackle any changes or obstacles that come your way. Little and often is the key to success!

Take a deep breath.
Inhale peace.
Exhale happiness.

A. D. Posey

MONEY MATTERS

To secure your financial future, have an agreed budget and savings strategy and stick to it. How much you see your future self overlapping with your current self is likely to reflect your attitude towards saving and for some people, their future self can seem very remote! To tackle this, look at your monthly expenditure and calculate how much you spend on necessities – things like housing, utilities, food and transport. What is left over is your discretionary income, which you can assign to non-essential things (such as going out, holidays and entertainment) and savings. Work out a general rule that is agreeable, such as a 60/40 or 80/20 split.

I will take
responsibility for
my future self

BE AN AMATEUR

One of the most important things in your best life should be something you love doing simply for the sake of doing it. More than anything else, a hobby doesn't require you to aim for perfection or look to complete it to a professional standard. Simply give yourself permission to be an amateur and not worry about the result. Often when you get good at a hobby you will notice it starts to put pressure on your schedule and feel a bit stressful – a bit like hard work! Find something else you can do that will put you in a flow state, help you relax and for which the outcome doesn't matter.

Ask yourself if what
you are doing today brings
you closer to where you
want to be tomorrow.

Anonymous

CHAPTER FOUR

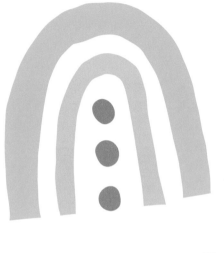

HOW TO LIVE YOUR BEST LIFE

In the previous chapters, you've hopefully found inspiration and practical tips for working out what your best life might look like, how to feel happy and comfortable in your own skin, and new ideas for making positive changes in your life. In this chapter, you will find suggestions for how to bring your values and goals together with your everyday life and how to set yourself up for a fulfilling future. The rest of your life starts today! Over the next few pages, you will discover how to stay on track and focus on the things that truly matter for living your best life.

SETTING GOOD GOALS

You know what you want your life to look like, so now is the time to work out how to fulfil your ambitions. To increase your chances of success you will need to set goals that work. Your personal goals should be SMART: Specific, Measurable, Achievable, Realistic and Time-bound.

Decide on the most important thing you want to achieve. If you want to improve your fitness, set a specific goal; maybe you decide you'd like to take up running. Next, decide how you're going to measure your progress. Will you be timing how long you can run for, or setting a distance?

Make sure it's achievable by breaking your goal into manageable smaller goals – if you're a novice runner, a 5K challenge is much more likely to be successful than a marathon. Be realistic and consider how this will fit into your everyday life. Running three times a week and achieving your goal over a couple of months is more realistic than deciding to run every day for three weeks.

Following this goal-orientated process means you're making an action plan to achieve an important objective that will really impact your life.

BE INTENTIONAL

When you do something intentionally, you do it with purpose. Once you're clear about the goals you're aiming for, many decisions in your life will become easier. Instead of wishful thinking, you will have an actionable plan that allows you to organize your days in a way that aligns with the overall vision of your best life. You're already thinking intentionally about it by reading this book. Starting each day with a clear intention is a powerful way to maintain a sense of control and purpose and will keep you on track for living your best life.

Do something today
that your future self
will thank you for.

Sean Patrick Flanery

PRIORITIZE

A priority means the most important thing. It comes from the Latin *prior*, meaning "before". This is a helpful way to remember that if something takes priority, it should come before all other things. You might often hear people talking about multiple priorities, but in the true sense of the word, you can't have more than one. If you have three priorities, which comes first? To stay focused on what matters, each morning ask yourself, "What is the most important thing to do today?" Getting the important things done first is the best way to manage your time effectively.

Put first
things first

Every time you learn a new skill, expose yourself to a new environment or try something new, your brain grows and makes new connections. Trying new things is beneficial for your personal growth too - you will get to know yourself better through new experiences. Not only that, but your ability to create your best life can only stem from the ways you add to it, or the tools at hand to change it. Your favourite music, foods, places and films are only so because once upon a time you gave them a go!

We tend to remember when we did something for the first time - trying new things makes memories. It's a great way to mark out time and look back over what you've accomplished. It's also a great way to stay motivated - too much repetition can get boring, so finding new ways to exercise or new meals to cook can make everyday life a bit more interesting. And as we often find new ideas on the borderline between the familiar and the new, it's also great for growing your creativity!

The greater danger for
most of us lies not in
setting our aim too high
and falling short,

but in setting our
aim too low and
achieving our mark.

Michelangelo

SELF-BELIEF

To live your best life, first you need
to know what you want and then
you need a plan to get it. The next
stage of successfully executing that
plan requires a number of skills and
attributes, all of which are underpinned
by self-belief. Self-belief isn't about
believing that you're right all the time
but about trusting in yourself to get
there eventually. It's about believing
in the worth of your values and goals
so that your purpose is always clear
and your intentions are always good.
Have confidence in your innate abilities
to learn, adapt and grow and you will
be well-equipped to succeed and find
fulfilment in every area of your life.

Trust yourself. You know
more than you think you do.

Benjamin Spock

STAYING MOTIVATED

Hopefully, right now you're full of determination to work on your goals and make positive changes. As time passes, it can be difficult to maintain your focus and momentum. Set monthly dates in a diary to check in with your values, asking yourself if you're living by them. Write down your goals and do a weekly review. If you've struggled one week, don't worry - that's just real life! Simply promise yourself to pick up again where you left off, this time with the knowledge that although you've been held up by metaphorical traffic, you're already miles from your starting point and travelling in the right direction.

Try something new
and you'll learn
something new

GROW YOUR MIND

Do you believe you have a certain amount of potential? We now know that the brain continues to grow and change throughout our lives - a phenomenon called neuroplasticity. This means that no one has a fixed level of intelligence - your brain is naturally designed for growth, which means your potential grows with you. Stanford psychologist Carol Dweck suggests that people who think their success is due to their innate abilities have a "fixed mindset" whereas people who think their success is due to learning, determination and hard work have a "growth mindset".

With a growth mindset, instead of thinking you can't do something, you think in terms of not being able to do it "yet" and focus on the process or steps required to learn how. Another difference between the two mindsets is how you react to failure. With a fixed mindset, you're likely to avoid challenges and give up easily due to a fear of failure, but with a growth mindset, you're not afraid to take on challenges and you see difficulty as being simply part of the growth process. Understanding these two mindsets can improve your self-awareness and help you make more informed choices to live your best life.

RESILIENCE

Grit, determination, the ability to bounce back after a setback: these are all part of being resilient. You can't always avoid stress coming into your life, but you can choose how you respond to it. Being resilient is about having a good response to challenging situations so you don't get overwhelmed and give up. It's about being flexible enough to adapt, determined enough to keep going and positive enough to believe you will get there in the end. Resilience is a vital skill that you can work on and grow and will strengthen your ability to make positive life changes stick.

Never give up then,
for that is just the
place and time that
the tide will turn.

Harriet Beecher Stowe

BE CURIOUS

One of the ways you can keep challenging yourself and pushing the boundaries is through your natural curiosity. Just as young children ask "why" when they are trying to find out how the world works, staying curious about new things helps you to continue learning throughout your life, which is proven to lead to greater life satisfaction and well-being. Curiosity isn't limited to wondering how something works or trying a new experience. For example, being curious about others can be a wonderful way of expanding your empathy and building relationships. By maintaining an enquiring mind you will stay engaged with the world around you.

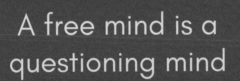

A free mind is a
questioning mind

AVOID PERFECTIONISM

It's easy to think that living your best life must somehow mean living a perfect life. Yet if you set yourself unrelenting standards to live up to, you will never be content. There are many causes of perfectionism: maybe you had parents with high standards and spent your childhood always trying to please them, or perhaps you have the feeling that in some way you're not quite enough. No one is perfect, so constantly trying to achieve perfection will leave you feeling as if you're always failing or falling short, as if your work is never done, and as if everything is just another task. Start by giving yourself permission to make mistakes. Try to accept that although your world may be imperfect, this will be massively outweighed by the sense of freedom you will get from setting yourself more realistic standards. Will that thing you're obsessing over really matter next year? Limit the amount of time you afford certain tasks so you don't spend too long in search of perfection when good enough will do. Most important of all, give yourself permission to relax!

Sometimes the smallest

step in the right direction

*ends up being the
biggest step of your life.*

Naeem Callaway

BE OPEN AND CLOSED

An open mind will open doors to a whole world of future possibilities you may not have considered. Five years from now you might have a job that hasn't been invented yet! To live a purposeful life you need to be selective – to shut out distractions and focus on your goals. However, at the same time, you need to keep your mind open enough to learn and iterate, tweaking your plans and changing route. Remember, the world is huge and so is your potential for growth. Practise switching between two types of thinking: opening up to widen your experience and closing down to achieve your goals.

You can do anything,
but you can't do everything

BE A GLOBAL CITIZEN

Do you think of yourself as part of a group? Schools, workplaces, football clubs, societies and nations can all give you a sense of identity but your identity goes beyond local groups and geographical boundaries when you think of yourself as belonging to humanity as a whole. Seen in this way, you're connected with every other human on the planet. The way you live your life, through the causes you support and the things you buy, can affect people living on the other side of the world. With this feeling of connectedness you can help make the world a fairer and better place.

I am part of
something amazing

AFFIRMATIONS

If you hear something often enough, you start to believe it. This is the idea behind practising simple affirmations every day. An affirmation is a positive statement – something that confirms your belief in yourself. With regular repetition, this positive thinking will become embedded in your subconscious. As you've been reading this book, what ideas have really stood out for you? Some ideas are: "I can learn to do anything." "I am grateful." "I am creative." You can create your own statement, starting with "I".

To make sure you do it every day, associate it with a frequent task. Write it on a sticky note and put it on the bathroom mirror so you can say it when you brush your teeth first thing in the morning and just before bed. Or put the sticky note on a cupboard where you keep your mugs, so you say it when you make your first drink of the day. Make sure your words align with your values and goals and it will be a powerful daily reminder to keep you on track.

Be mindful.
Be grateful.
Be positive.
Be true. Be kind.

Roy T. Bennett